20TH CENTURY ART

1910-20

THE BIRTH OF ABSTRACT ART

Please visit our web site at: www.garethstevens.com
For a free color catalog describing Gareth Stevens' list of high-quality books
and multimedia programs, call 1-800-542-2595 (USA) or 1-800-461-9120 (Canada).
Gareth Stevens Publishing's Fax: (414) 332-3567.

Library of Congress Cataloging-in-Publication Data available upon request from publisher.
Fax (414) 336-0157 for the attention of the Publishing Records Department.

ISBN 0-8368-2849-6

This North American edition first published in 2001 by
Gareth Stevens Publishing
A World Almanac Education Group Company
330 West Olive Street, Suite 100
Milwaukee, WI 53212 USA

Original edition © 2000 by David West Children's Books. First published in Great Britain in 2000 by
Heinemann Library, Halley Court, Jordan Hill, Oxford OX2 8EJ, a division of Reed Educational and
Professional Publishing Limited. This U.S. edition © 2001 by Gareth Stevens, Inc. Additional end
matter © 2001 by Gareth Stevens, Inc.

Picture Research: Brooks Krikler Research
Picture Editor: Carlotta Cooper
Gareth Stevens Editor: Catherine Gardner

Photo Credits:
Abbreviations: (t) top, (m) middle, (b) bottom, (l) left, (r) right

AKG London: pages 3, 6(t), 7(t), 9(b), 10(l), 11(b), 16(t), 18(t), 19(m, br), 21(t, bl), 23.
AKG London © DACS 2000: pages 25(b), 28, 29(m).
Alitalia: page 8(t).
Bridgeman Art Library: pages 8(b), 12(r), 13(b), 17(t).
Bridgeman Art Library © 2000 Mondrian/Holtzman Trust c/o Beeldrecht, Amsterdam, Holland,
    and DACS, London: page 25(t).
Bridgeman Art Library © ADAGP, Paris, and DACS, London, 2000: cover, pages 6(b), 10(r),
    11(t), 22(b), 26(b).
Bridgeman Art Library © DACS 2000: pages 5, 13(t), 20.
Corbis: pages 4(t), 7(b), 15, 26(t).
Corbis © ADAGP, Paris, and DACS, London, 2000: page 19(bl).
Corbis © Archivo Icongrafico, S.A.: page 9(t).
Tom Donovan Military Books: page 4(b).
Mary Evans Picture Library: page 21(br).
Haags Gemeentemuseum, Netherlands/Bridgeman Art Library: page 24(r).
Imperial War Museum, London/Bridgeman Art Library: page 16(b).
Solution Pictures: page 17(b).
Frank Spooner Pictures: pages 12(l), 24-25(b), 29(t, b).
Stapleton Collection UK/Bridgeman Art Library: pages 14(t), 18(b).
Stedelijk Museum, Amsterdam, Netherlands/Bridgeman Art Library: page 27.
© Tate London 2000: page 14(b).

Printed in the United States of America

1 2 3 4 5 6 7 8 9 05 04 03 02 01

20TH CENTURY ART

1910-20

THE BIRTH OF ABSTRACT ART

Jackie Gaff

Gareth Stevens Publishing
A WORLD ALMANAC EDUCATION GROUP COMPANY

CONTENTS

Scientific discoveries affected art between 1910 and 1920. Physicists Ernest Rutherford and Niels Bohr (above) *showed that the atom was not the basic unit of matter, but a moving bundle of smaller particles. "The disintegration of the atom," wrote Kandinsky in 1913, "was to me like the disintegration of the whole world."*

TURBULENT TIMES

Among the many events that shook the world in the years 1910 to 1920, World War I (1914–1918) was by far the most destructive. It was the first war fought on land, at sea, and in the air, and it was the most shocking war people had ever experienced. As many as 10 million soldiers and almost the same number of civilians died in the war.

In the world of art during these years, a new and very different style developed. Total abstraction, as it was called, did not attempt to represent, or show, real scenes, people, or objects.

The leading pioneers of abstract art included Dutch-born Piet Mondrian (1872–1944) and Russian-born Kasimir Malevich (1878–1935) and Vasily Kandinsky (1866–1944). A friend of Kandinsky, Swiss-German artist Paul Klee (1879–1940), expressed the feeling of his generation when he said in 1915, "The more terrifying the world becomes . . . the more art becomes abstract."

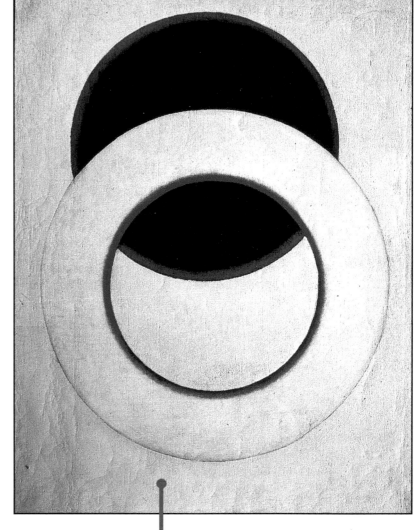

WHITE CIRCLE,
Alexander Rodchenko, 1918

Totally abstract paintings are made up of lines, shapes, and colors that exist for their own sake, not to describe or suggest something else. The first geometric abstract art was created in Russia just before World War I.

5

World War I was the first time two new inventions, airplanes and tanks, were used as weapons. The first powered flight took place in 1903, and the tank first saw action in 1916.

CUBIST CONSTRUCTIONS

Although they did not choose to use total abstraction, Spaniard Pablo Picasso (1881–1973) and Frenchman Georges Braque (1882–1963) laid the foundations for it. In 1907, they began to develop the fragmented art style known as Cubism. In the years before the war, Picasso and Braque explored Cubism and gathered followers, including Spanish-born artist Juan Gris (1887–1927).

6

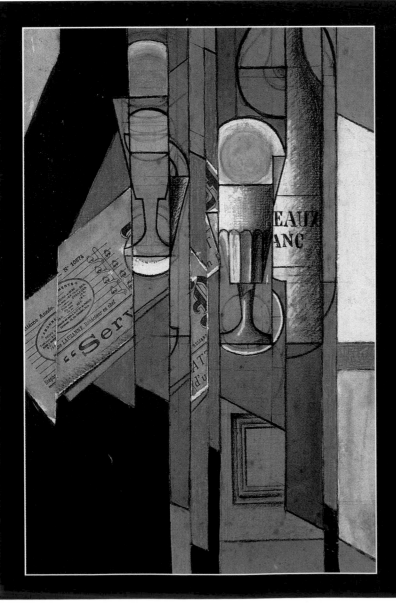

Gris was only forty years old when he died of kidney failure.

GLASSES, NEWSPAPER AND A BOTTLE OF WINE
JUAN GRIS, 1913

Gris moved from Spain to France in 1906, when he was nineteen. In Montmartre, a suburb of Paris, he rented a room in the same building as Picasso. He began painting seriously in 1910 and was soon seen as one of Picasso's and Braque's most brilliant followers. He quickly adopted new Cubist techniques, such as collage, and made them his own. In the collage *Glasses, Newspaper and a Bottle of Wine*, he used a technique called *papier collé*, which is French for "glued paper," because the only materials in it are pieces of paper. Cubists also made three-dimensional collages that were part painting and part sculpture, using materials such as fabric, wood, and nails.

SHATTERED ILLUSIONS

Cubism was a new way of depicting people, objects, and landscapes. Cubists did not create the traditional, mirrorlike illusion of three dimensions. Instead, they broke apart their subjects and put them back together to show them from all angles at once, like pieces of broken glass.

GLUING THE PIECES TOGETHER

By 1912, Picasso and Braque entered a new stage of Cubism. Rather than break down their subjects, they began to build their subjects up, making colleges on canvas using real objects. In *Still Life with Chair Caning* (1912), Picasso glued on a piece of oilcloth printed to look like the lattice-work caning on a chair seat. Picasso and Braque did not invent collage; it had long been used to make scrapbooks, for example. They were, however, the first to make collage an important part of fine art.

During his long working life, French artist Fernand Léger (1881–1955) tried many different art styles, always making them his own. After 1910, he developed an individual form of Cubism and was nicknamed a "tubist" because he used bold tube shapes.

COMING TO AMERICA

American photographer and art critic Alfred Stieglitz (1864–1946) played a vital role in introducing modern European art to the United States through his 291 Gallery, which opened in 1905. He also supported progressive American artists, such as Arthur Dove (1880–1946) and Georgia O'Keeffe (1887–1986), who married Stieglitz in 1924. Early in 1913, the influential Armory Show in New York City gave average Americans their first real look at modern art. More than 300,000 people paid to see hundreds of paintings and sculptures by American artists and avant-garde Europeans, such as Picasso and Braque.

Stieglitz supported avant-garde American artists through his 291 Gallery on New York's Fifth Avenue. It included exhibitions of Georgia O'Keeffe's work.

CUBISM IN COLOR

Before the war, the palettes of Picasso, Braque, and Gris leaned heavily toward brown and gray. Meanwhile, other artists explored a more colorful form of Cubism. While Picasso, Braque, and Gris concentrated on still lifes, the colorful Cubists tried to capture the speed and energy of modern city life.

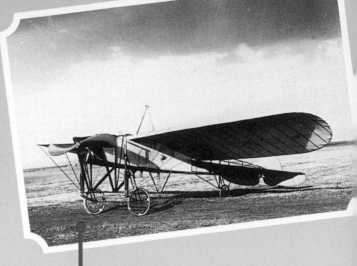

MODERN ART FOR A MODERN AGE

Beginning in 1909, French artist Robert Delaunay (1885–1941) created a series of colorful Cubist paintings of Paris and new inventions he considered to be miracles of modern engineering, including airplanes and the Eiffel Tower. Reaching a height of 984 feet (300 meters), the Eiffel Tower had become the world's tallest building when it was completed in 1889.

The Wright brothers achieved powered flight for the first time in 1903. One of the amazing scientific advances of the early 20th century, flight became a symbol of modern life. Delaunay included airplanes in many of his paintings. His Homage to Blériot, 1914, was dedicated to the French aviator Louis Blériot, who in 1909 became the first person to fly across the English Channel.

8

MAKING AN IMPRESSION

Delaunay admired the artists of the 19th century, such as Claude Monet (1840–1926) and other Impressionists, who had created new ways of painting. Like them, he studied the science of light and color and was fascinated by the "law of simultaneous contrasts." According to this rule, the differences between two colors appear greatest when the colors are placed next to each other. For example, orange looks redder when placed beside green. In his own paintings, Delaunay used the law of simultaneous contrasts to create movement and rhythm.

HAYSTACKS AT SUNSET, FROSTY WEATHER, *Claude Monet, 1891*

THE RUGBY TEAM
ROBERT DELAUNAY, 1912–1913

The Delaunays were among the first to create totally abstract works, but they also continued to make representational paintings. This one is full of symbols of movement and modern life: sports, an airplane, the Eiffel Tower, and a ferris wheel. "Astra" was the name of an aircraft company and is the Latin word for "stars."

MARRIAGE OF MINDS

Delaunay and his wife, Russian-born artist Sonia Delaunay-Terk (1885–1979), developed an interest in color and movement. By 1912, they were painting totally abstract works, in which color and shape existed only for their own sake, not to represent objects. Describing abstract paintings, such as his *Circular Forms* series, Robert said, "Color is form and subject. It is the sole theme that is developed." The Delaunays called their abstract works "pure paintings." French poet and art critic Guillaume Apollinaire (1880–1918) called the works "Orphic Cubism" — "Orphism," for short. He created the word "Orphic" from Orpheus, the musician of ancient Greek and Roman myth whose music was said to be so beautiful that even rivers stopped flowing to listen to it.

Apollinaire defined Orphism as "the art of painting new structures out of elements that have not been borrowed from the visual sphere, but have been created entire by the artist himself."

VASILY KANDINSKY

Kandinsky was born in 1866 in Russia, where he studied law and economics. He was thirty when he decided to train as a painter and moved to Munich, Germany, one of Europe's main artistic centers at that time. He became one of the three key figures in the development of abstract art.

In 1911, Kandinsky and German artists Franz Marc (1880–1916) and Gabrielle Münter (1877–1962) started an avant-garde group they named Der Blaue Reiter, which is German for "the blue rider." The group held two exhibitions before it was broken up by World War I.

10

MOMENTS OF TRUTH

Kandinsky said he had several major turning points in his artistic life. The first one happened when he saw one of Monet's series of haystack paintings (*page 8*), which inspired him to take up art in 1896. The second turning point took place in 1909, when he found an incredibly beautiful painting in his studio in which he could see "nothing but shapes and colors." He soon realized it was one of his own paintings, turned on its side, but the experience led him to explore abstraction.

COMPOSITION VII
VASILY KANDINSKY, 1913

Colors, shapes, and lines collide and explode in this energetic painting. Its main theme is the death and rebirth of the universe. Kandinsky moved gradually toward total abstraction after 1910, and some of the paintings from this time have references to the real world, like the symbol for a boat with three oars (*bottom left corner*). After World War I, his style became more geometric, with intersecting circles, triangles, and squares.

In 1909, Kandinsky and Gabrielle Münter moved into their second home in the village of Murnau, in the foothills of the Alps. This photograph was taken while Kandinsky was working in the garden there.

THE MUSIC OF PAINTING

Kandinsky aimed to reveal spiritual truths through his art. He believed that, like music, abstract art could appeal to the soul, not just the eyes. "Color is the keyboard, the eyes are the hammers, the soul is the piano with many strings," he wrote. He also developed a vocabulary of color to define the unique properties of individual colors. For example, red gave "the impression of a strong drum beat," while yellow sounded "like a high-pitched trumpet."

MUSIC FOR THE MODERN AGE

Musicians also began to break with the past after 1910. One of the most innovative composers was Austrian Arnold Schoenberg (1874– 1951). At the time, his use of dissonance, or lack of harmony, and atonality, or music not written in a particular key, left most audiences puzzled or even hostile. Kandinsky, however, became an admirer and close friend of Schoenberg. Schoenberg was also a painter and exhibited with Der Blaue Reiter group.

Arnold Schoenberg

FUTURISM

The most vocal art movement of the period was Futurism, founded in 1909 by Italian poet Filippo Tommaso Marinetti (1876–1944). Marinetti hated the past and loved the modern — and nothing symbolized modern life more for him than speed!

"We declare that the splendour of the world has been enriched with a new form of beauty, the beauty of speed. A racing car . . . is more beautiful than the Victory of Samothrace *[a famous ancient Greek sculpture],"* wrote Marinetti.

OUT WITH THE OLD

Marinetti loved the speed and activity of new inventions, such as electricity, trains, cars, and airplanes. He saw museums as monuments to traditional art and wanted to tear them down. He glorified chaos and destruction and claimed "beauty now exists only in struggle."

UNIQUE FORMS OF CONTINUITY IN SPACE
UMBERTO BOCCIONI, 1913

Boccioni was a sculptor as well as a painter. This dramatically striding figure is one of his most impressive works. As it sweeps forward, he said, it carries "blocks of atmosphere" along with it. Boccioni was influenced by the sculptures of Picasso and Constantin Brancusi (1876–1957). He wanted to bring new life to the "mummified art" of the past and use untraditional materials such as glass, mirror, electric lights, and motors, to create art.

12

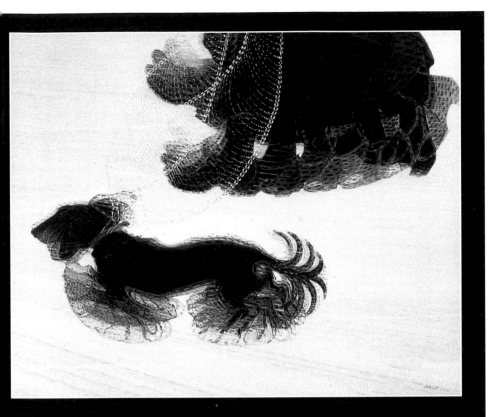

DYNAMISM OF A DOG ON A LEASH
GIACOMO BALLA, 1912

Balla wasn't interested in machines and violence, and his paintings were gently beautiful or funny. In this painting, the wagging tail and trotting legs of a dachshund look as if they were photographed in motion.

IN WITH THE NEW

Marinetti was a poet, not a painter. Artists who joined his Futurist movement had to find a way to deal with his ideas in art. They included Italian artists Giacomo Balla (1871–1958), Umberto Boccioni (1882–1916), Carlo Carrà (1881–1966), Luigi Russolo (1885–1947), and Gino Severini (1883–1966) and architect Antonio Sant'Elia (1888–1916). Although their individual styles differed, these Futurists shared the search for a way to express speed and energy. They experimented with a variety of different art styles, including Cubism. Eventually, many of them used a version of Orphism.

13

GALLOPING HORSE, *Eadweard Muybridge, 1887*

MOVING PICTURES

Some Futurists saw photography as a lesser art. Many other Futurists, however, were influenced by the series of photographs of motion taken in the 1880s by Eadweard Muybridge (1830–1904) in Britain and Étienne-Jules Marey (1830–1903) in France. Italian photographer Anton Giulio Bragaglia (1890–1960), who was linked to the Futurists, experimented with long exposures of photographic film to create beautiful blurred images of moving people. Bragaglia called these images "photodynamic."

VORTICISM

With the publication of a magazine called *BLAST*, a group of British artists and writers launched a new style, called Vorticism, in July 1914. Vorticism evolved out of Cubism and Futurism. The beginning of World War I soon ended the group's activities, and by late 1915, its members had scattered and gone their own ways.

COVER OF BLAST MAGAZINE, *Wyndham Lewis, 1915*

There were only two issues of BLAST. The second was published in July 1915, a month after the only Vorticist exhibition.

14

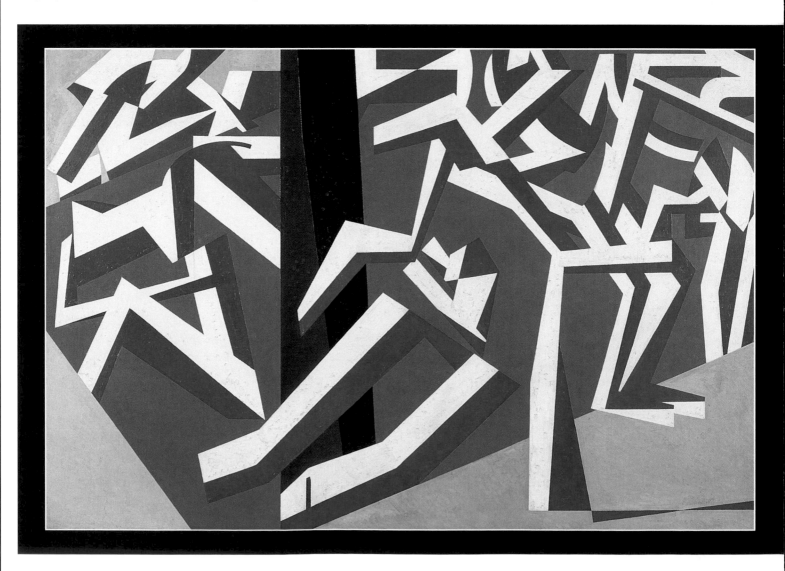

THE MUD BATH
DAVID BOMBERG, c. 1913–1914

British artist David Bomberg (1890–1957) turned down an invitation to join the Vorticist group. The energy and jagged, semi-abstract shapes of works like *The Mud Bath*, however, are among the finest examples of the effects Vorticists were trying to create. At first glance, Bomberg's painting may appear totally abstract, but it actually shows blue and white bathers leaping around a red rectangle of water. Bomberg based the painting on sketches made at public baths in the Whitechapel area of London's East End, where he grew up.

CLUB MEMBERSHIP
The first issue of *BLAST* featured a manifesto, or statement of the group's views. It was signed by British writer and painter Wyndham Lewis (1882–1957), who edited *BLAST*, and other avant-garde artists, such as Britons Jessica Dismorr (1885–1939), William Roberts (1895–1980), and Edward Wadsworth (1889–1949); Frenchman Henri Gaudier-Brzeska (1891–1915); and American poet Ezra Pound (1885–1972).

DEEP AND MEANINGFUL
Like Orphists and Futurists, Vorticists aimed to celebrate the energy of modern life through abstract and semi-abstract art. Their style, however, was far more jagged. Pound, who said he invented the group's name, noted the main difference in Vorticism when he described Futurism as "a spreading, or surface art, as opposed to Vorticism, which is intensive," meaning concentrated, with a sense of depth. The group's name came from the word "vortex," which means a whirling and sucking motion. Looking at a Vorticist painting is almost like peering into a dark, endless pit or a black hole in space.

ARTISTS AT WAR

The start of World War I in August 1914 broke up artistic communities in European cities like Paris and Munich. While some artists lived in neutral nations and did not fight, others joined the military or were drafted. Many artists died, including Futurists Boccioni and Sant'Elia; Vorticist Gaudier-Brzeska; and Marc, one of the founders of Der Blaue Reiter.

Marc was killed in the Battle of Verdun in March 1916.

A BATTERY SHELLED, WYNDHAM LEWIS, 1919

Three officers stand on the sidelines while their men work to clear the destruction of a bomb attack. Lewis was working from firsthand experience; he served as a gunner before he became an official war artist in 1917. Lewis toned down his abstract Vorticist style during the war not only because of official restrictions, but also because of his experiences. "The geometrics which had interested me so before, I now felt were bleak and empty," he said.

16

Many artists produced propaganda posters that persuaded men to join the military and fight.

ARTISTS AT THE FRONT

Australia, Britain, Canada, and the United States set up official war artist plans. Under these plans, artists were recruited to record the events of the war for national records. They also produced propaganda, or posters and other materials that encouraged public support of the war effort. Official war artists included men who were either too old for active duty or who had been injured and sent home. Only these artists could work at the front lines. Women served as official war artists at home.

TERROR IN THE TRENCHES

Many new weapons were introduced during the war, and military commanders were slow to respond. For the first time, soldiers in the trenches were exposed to poison gas, flame-throwers, and bombs dropped from airplanes. Soldiers, armed only with bayonets, faced machine-gun fire from the newly invented tank. As many as 10 million soldiers died.

British front line, Battle of the Somme, 1916

PAINTING PART OF THE PICTURE

These artists had to follow rules on subject matter and style. In Britain, for example, total abstraction was not allowed. As a result, many of the best artistic responses to the horror of the war came after the peace of 1918.

DADA

Anti-art, anti-sense, anti-tradition, anti-modern life, anti-war — Dada was anti-everything!

WORLD AT WAR

The brutality of the war made some people lose faith in the governments and society responsible for waging it. The Dada art movement was intended to show disgust for the so-called civilized humans who had acted like such barbarians. Dada art was deliberately absurd. It rejected traditional ideas and standards in all the arts — from music and poetry to painting and performance.

18

As the war ended, Dada grew popular in German artistic centers. A dummy hung in this Berlin gallery had the head of a pig and was dressed in a German officer's uniform. A sign on it read, "Hanged by the Revolution."

SWISS EYE OF THE STORM

During the war, many avant-garde writers and artists moved to the neutral country of Switzerland. European Dada was started there, in Zurich, in 1916. The artists who created the Dada movement included German Hugo Ball (1886–1927), Frenchman Hans Arp (1887–1966), and Romanian Tristan Tzara (1896–1963).

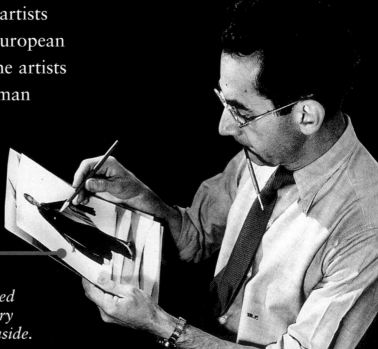

American artist, photographer, and film-maker Man Ray was a leader of New York Dada. In 1921, he moved to Paris. For his first Dada event there, he filled a gallery with balloons that viewers had to pop to find the art inside.

FOUNTAIN
MARCEL DUCHAMP, 1917

A urinal laid on its back and signed R. Mutt — is this art? Few people thought so at the time, and many people would ask the same question today. Duchamp used ready-made objects like this to challenge traditional ideas and widen the definition of art. He made it possible for the ideas behind a work of art to be as important as the act of creating it. Technical skill was no longer most important. Choosing an object for display could be just as significant. Only the ideas mattered.

"Whether Mr. Mutt with his own hands made the fountain or not has no importance. He chose it . . . . created a new thought for that object," Duchamp explained.

SCATTERING CHAOS

Dada spread through Europe quickly. It developed separately in New York, where it was led by French-born Marcel Duchamp (1887–1968) and Francis Picabia (1879–1953) and American Man Ray (1890–1976). Dada's focus on chaos and nonsense had a huge effect on 20th-century art. It led to the birth of several other art movements, including the dreamlike Surrealism of the 1920s and 1930s.

THEATRE OF THE ABSURD

The center of Dada in Zurich was Hugo Ball's Cabaret Voltaire. "Happenings" there included the chanting of nonsense poems, such as Ball's "Karawane," which went "zimzim urallala zimzim zanzibar . . ." The poems often were drowned out by "noise music" made by thumping drums, bottles, and anything else that was handy.

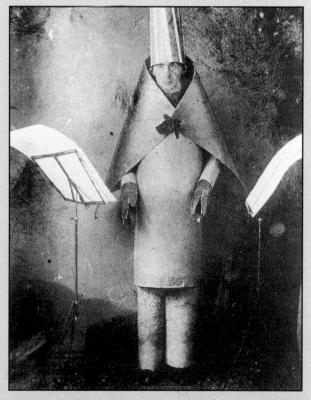

Hugo Ball reciting "Karawane" in 1916.

DE CHIRICO'S METAPHYSICAL PAINTING

The mysterious and dreamlike paintings produced by Greek-born Italian Giorgio de Chirico (1888–1978) were almost as bizarre as the creations made by the Dadaists. Like Dada, De Chirico's style would influence the birth of Surrealism in the 1920s. De Chirico called his art style Metaphysical Painting. He used the word *metaphysical* to mean "puzzling" and to describe a feeling of separation from reality. His metaphysical effects make his works appear strange, shocking, and sometimes sinister.

MELANCHOLY
GIORGIO DE CHIRICO, C. 1912

De Chirico painted mysteriously empty city squares like this one, edged by buildings and rows of arches, with long, dark shadows. There often are no people in the painting, just classical statues or faceless dummies. The perspective, or the sense of depth and distance, is exaggerated or twisted. In this work, for example, the statue is tilted, but the ground is flat. The sense of time is confusing, as well — is the painting set in the past, the present, or the future? The buildings suggest the past, but in many paintings a tiny modern steam train puffs across a distant horizon. Some of de Chirico's images simply express sadness and loneliness, while others produce feelings of fear and isolation.

MELANCONIA

20

LEARNING FROM THE PAST

De Chirico was not interested in Cubism or Futurism. Instead of turning his back on history, he embraced the classical art of Greek and Roman times. Rather than follow Cubists who were working to break the illusion of three dimensions, de Chirico adapted and twisted the laws of perspective.

The Surrealists admired the work de Chirico produced between 1910 and 1920.

MEETING OF METAPHYSICAL MINDS

De Chirico began to develop his style when he lived in Paris. After the war broke out, he was drafted into the Italian army and sent to the city of Ferrara in northern Italy. In 1917, while in Ferrara, de Chirico met Carlo Carrà. Carrà was once a Futurist, but his faith in the art of the past had been restored, and he was a quick convert to de Chirico's style. Carrá helped de Chirico launch Metaphysical Painting as an art movement. Their friendship, however, was short-lived and ended in a quarrel in 1919.

Like de Chirico, Russian-born Marc Chagall (1887–1985) also influenced the Surrealists. Chagall created fairy-tale images of flying horses and musicians floating through the air.

After the Industrial Revolution of the 19th century, many people moved from farms to cities to find work in factories. This movement sparked the rapid growth of cities and towns. With such rapid growth, the city came to be seen as a place of alienation, where a person feels alone even when in a crowd. This feeling comes through in de Chirico's paintings. In literature, it was expressed by American-born Briton T.S. Eliot (1888–1965) in his great poem *The Waste Land*. Loaded with references to the literature of the past, the poem also questions the values of the present.

T.S. Eliot's The Waste Land *caused an uproar when it was published in 1922. Some critics called it a masterpiece and others, a hoax.*

MODIGLIANI

Like de Chirico and Carrà, Amedeo Modigliani (1884–1920) also admired the great works of the past. Born in Italy, Modigliani moved to Paris in 1906 and spent the rest of his short life there.

BOHEMIAN RHAPSODY

Shortly after arriving in Paris, Modigliani settled in the Montparnasse district. This area, as well as nearby Montmartre, attracted many artists and writers to Paris in the early 20th century. Modigliani threw himself into a wild and self-destructive lifestyle with the same passion he had for art. He was addicted to drugs and alcohol and once said, "I am going to drink myself to death." Weakened by his way of life, he died from a combination of pneumonia and tubercular meningitis.

PUTTING WOMEN IN THE PICTURE

Russian-born painter Maria Vorobeva (1892–1984) was known as Marevna, a nickname given to her after she left Russia to study painting in Italy and France. Between 1910 and 1920, Marevna moved in the same social circles as Modigliani, and she painted this portrait in the 1960s in memory of friendships made during

HOMAGE TO FRIENDS FROM MONTPARNASSE, *Marevna, 1961*

JEANNE HÉBUTERNE
Amedeo modigliani, 1919

Modigliani was inspired by the art of the past, but, unlike this art, he did not choose to depict the real world. Instead he tried to express more spiritual and universal themes. In July 1917, Modigliani met Jeanne Hébuterne, the woman portrayed in this painting. They had a child late in 1918, and she was pregnant with a second child when this portrait was painted. She was devoted to Modigliani and committed suicide two days after he died. In this painting, Jeanne's expression is blank and her pale blue eyes are empty. Modigliani did not want to make her personality the chief subject of the painting. Instead he transformed her into a symbol of sad resignation.

that time. On the left are Marevna and her daughter, Marika. Behind Marevna is Marika's father, Mexican artist Diego Rivera (1886–1957). Modigliani is in the center of the painting, with Jeanne Hébuterne behind his raised glass. Women artists faced many challenges in those days, Marevna said. "For a man the problem is easier to solve: he nearly always has a woman, wife or mistress, who earns money. . . . She is devoted, and sacrifices herself until the man becomes celebrated."

STUDENT OF A MODERN MASTER

Modigliani's finest works were the beautiful portraits and nudes he painted in the last five years of his life. He was influenced by the simplified forms of the sculptor Constantin Brancusi, whom he met in 1909. He worked mainly on sculpture until the war stopped his supply of materials and forced him to return to painting and drawing.

HEIR TO AN OLD MASTER

Modigliani depicted women with a simple, elegant style. The great 15th-century Italian painter Sandro Botticelli (*c.* 1445–1510) portrayed women with similar grace, and Modigliani is often described as his artistic heir.

SELF-PORTRAIT, 1920

Modigliani was a fine draftsman and could capture his subject with a few simple strokes of pencil.

23

PIET MONDRIAN

Dutch-born artist Piet Mondrian (1872–1944) was one of the three key figures in the development of total abstraction. He was matched in importance only by Kandinsky and Russian Kasimir Malevich (1878–1935).

DEAD END STREET

Mondrian arrived in Paris in 1912, at the age of forty. Until then, his subjects had been mainly landscapes. He experimented with Cubism for a while, but he soon said that it was "not developing abstraction toward its own goal, the expression of pure reality."

ROAD TO ENLIGHTENMENT

Like Kandinsky, Mondrian was searching for a way to create art that would rise above the material world and express universal truths. He thought art should provide "a transition to the finer regions, which I shall call the spiritual realm."

COMPOSITION WITH RED, BLUE AND YELLOW
PIET MONDRIAN, 1930

For Mondrian, the pure colors and straight lines of his paintings expressed the absolute harmony of the universe. Influenced by the mystical philosophies of his day, he believed that his horizontal and vertical grids reached a balance between such elements as the feminine and the masculine, negative and positive, and stillness and movement. Straight lines were not his only passion, however — he also loved jazz music and dancing!

PORTRAIT OF PIET MONDRIAN, *M. Elout-Drabbe, 1915*

24

FINDING A NEW DIRECTION

Mondrian went back to the Netherlands in 1914 to visit his sick father, but the start of the war kept him from returning to Paris. During this time, his paintings became increasingly abstract, and he discovered his own individual style. By the early 1920s, he had arrived at a totally abstract, geometric style, which he continued to explore until his death. The only shapes he used were squares and rectangles, and the only colors were the three primary colors — red, yellow, and blue — plus black and white and, occasionally, gray.

Mondrian's love of horizontal and vertical lines grew in part from the flatness of the Dutch landscape, which was crisscrossed by a grid of canals.

In 1915, Mondrian met Dutch artist and writer Theo van Doesburg (1883–1931) and converted him to geometric abstraction. Two years later, van Doesburg started a magazine, as well as a group of artists and architects. He named them both *De Stijl*, which is Dutch for "the style." They both were very influential in launching a simple style of design, which used geometric shapes in everything from furniture to houses.

DESIGN FOR UNIVERSITY HALL, *Theo van Doesburg, 1923*

MALEVICH AND SUPREMATISM

The first totally abstract geometric painting was a simple black square on a white background. The artist who made it was Russian Kasimir Malevich. Although Malevich claimed that he created the work in 1913, the exact date cannot be proved. The first time it was seen in public was at an exhibition in December 1915 in the Russian city of St. Petersburg.

REACHING HIGHER GROUND

Malevich showed thirty-nine abstract works at this exhibition, all consisting of flat geometric shapes on plain backgrounds. He named his radical new style Suprematism. He took the term from the word *supremacy*, which means "the state of being of the highest quality or of utmost importance."

American Robert Goddard designed the first liquid-fuel rocket (above), *which was launched in 1926. Space science and the idea of space travel fascinated Malevich.*

26

LEADING LIGHTS

Other leaders of Russian avant-garde art in the years before the war included Natalia Goncharova (1881–1962) and Mikhail Larionov (1881–1964). Like Malevich, they worked in a style called Cubo-Futurism. This style combined the Cubist idea of breaking up a subject into fragments, or pieces, with the Futurist fascination with speed and modern city life. All three artists also wanted to develop styles that depended less on Western European influences and more on Eastern European traditions, such as folk art and religious icon painting. Goncharova and Larionov left Russia in 1915 and settled in Paris in 1919.

THE CYCLIST, *Natalia Goncharova, 1912–13*

UNTITLED (SUPREMATIST PAINTING)
Kasimir Malevich, 1915

Malevich said these kinds of colored geometric forms on their simple white background carried him "into an endless emptiness, where all around you sense the creative nodes of the universe."

PURITY OF FORM

Before Malevich pioneered Suprematism, he had tried Cubism and Futurism. He had grown dissatisfied, however, with the way they still carried what he described as "the burden" of representing objects. If his art was to be purely non-representational, Malevich had to find images that do not exist in the natural world. This was where geometry came in. Pure geometric shapes, such as squares and rectangles, do not exist in nature. They only exist in our minds.

PURITY OF THOUGHT

Malevich was a devout Christian, but, like Kandinsky and Mondrian, he also had mystical beliefs. He said he wanted his abstract art to give insights into the "cosmic infinite" and to express "the supremacy of pure feeling." In 1918, he began a series of white-on-white paintings — white forms on white backgrounds. These were abstracts to end all abstracts. After he produced these extreme abstracts, however, he returned to representational art.

CONSTRUCTIVISM

The early years of the 20th century were a time of political unrest in Russia. The country's turmoil climaxed in the Revolution of 1917. The Russian ruler, Czar Nicholas II, was overthrown and replaced by a new Communist government.

DOWN WITH FINE ART

Russia's political revolution was accompanied by a revolution in the arts. One group of Russian artists, called the Constructivists, said it was outdated to think that fine arts, such as painting and sculpture, were better than applied arts, such as furniture and textile design, typography, ceramics, and metalworking.

UP WITH TECHNOLOGY

Constructivists believed artists should serve society. They felt artists should learn industrial design and make useful objects. Varvara Stepanova (1894–1958) and her husband, Alexander Rodchenko (1891–1956), were two of the main leaders of the movement. In 1920, they proclaimed, "Down with art! Up with technology!"

28

Rodchenko created Suprematist works between 1910 and 1920, but he then left easel painting for Constructivism. "The art of the future will not be the cozy decoration of family homes," he explained. During the 1920s, he turned to design and photography and worked on everything from furniture and interiors to advertising and propaganda posters. Posters were the chief method of spreading the Communist message to the public, and thousands of them were designed and printed after the Revolution.

CONSTRUCTION OF THE USSR
ALEXANDER RODCHENKO, 1920

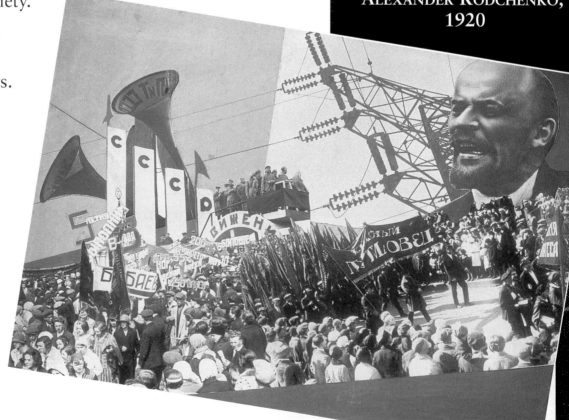

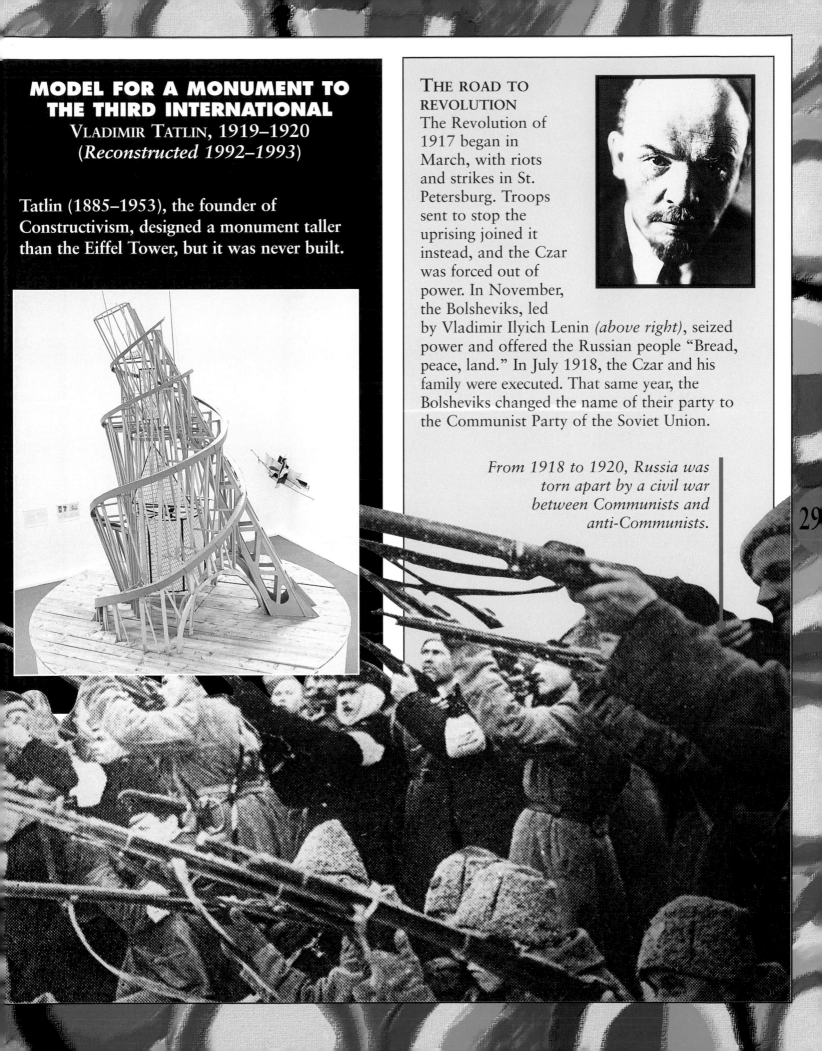

MODEL FOR A MONUMENT TO THE THIRD INTERNATIONAL
VLADIMIR TATLIN, 1919–1920
(*Reconstructed 1992–1993*)

Tatlin (1885–1953), the founder of Constructivism, designed a monument taller than the Eiffel Tower, but it was never built.

THE ROAD TO REVOLUTION

The Revolution of 1917 began in March, with riots and strikes in St. Petersburg. Troops sent to stop the uprising joined it instead, and the Czar was forced out of power. In November, the Bolsheviks, led by Vladimir Ilyich Lenin *(above right)*, seized power and offered the Russian people "Bread, peace, land." In July 1918, the Czar and his family were executed. That same year, the Bolsheviks changed the name of their party to the Communist Party of the Soviet Union.

From 1918 to 1920, Russia was torn apart by a civil war between Communists and anti-Communists.

· T I M E L I N E ·

	ART	WORLD EVENTS	DESIGN	THEATER & FILM	BOOKS & MUSIC
1910	•*Kandinsky paints abstract watercolors* •*London: Fry's first Post-Impressionist exhibition*	•*Union of South Africa founded* •*Japan takes control of Korea*	•*Adolf Loos' Modernist Steiner House in Vienna* •*Gropius and Meyer's Fagus shoe factory*	•*New York: Fanny Brice in the* Ziegfeld Follies •*Paris: Russian Ballet's* Schéhérazade *and* The Firebird	•*Igor Stravinsky composes music for* The Firebird •*E. M. Forster:* Howards End
1911	•*Der Blaue Reiter group formed in Berlin* •*Kandinsky's* On the Spiritual in Art *published*	•*Chinese revolution; Sun Yat Sen establishes republic* •*Amundsen reaches South Pole*	•*Brussels: Hoffmann's Palais Stoclet completed; interior mosaics by Gustav Klimt*	•*Cartoonist Winsor McCay's film,* Little Nemo •*Edward Knoblock's play,* Kismet	•*Irving Berlin: "Alexander's Ragtime Band"* •*Richard Strauss:* Der Rosenkavalier
1912	•*Picasso and Braque create first collages* •*Delaunays paint totally abstract works*	•*Balkan Wars (to 1913)* •*Titanic sinks on its maiden voyage, with loss of 1,500 people*	•*Electric blanket invented*	•*Keystone comedy studio founded by Mack Sennett* •*Guazzoni's silent film epic,* Quo Vadis	•*Carl Jung:* The Psychology of the Unconscious •*Richard Strauss:* Der Rosenkavalier
1913	•*U.S.: Armory Show of modern European art* •*Boccioni:* Unique Forms of Continuity in Space	•*Niels Bohr's quantum theory of the structure of the atom published*	•*Cass Gilbert's gothic-style skyscraper, the Woolworth Building, completed in New York*	•*U.S.: film studios first set up in Hollywood* •*George Bernard Shaw:* Pygmalion	•*Proust:* Swann's Way •*D. H. Lawrence:* Sons and Lovers
1914	•BLAST *magazine launches Vorticism* •*Bomberg:* The Mud Bath	•*Assassination of Austrian Archduke Ferdinand triggers World War I*	•*Italy: Antonio Sant'Elia's designs for a Futurist City, Città Nuova* •*Zipper invented*	•*Charlie Chaplin's tramp appears in* Kid Auto Races •*Mack Sennett:* Tillie's Punctured Romance	•*Gustav Holst:* The Planets *(to 1917)* •*James Joyce's short stories,* Dubliners
1915	•*Malevich publishes his Suprematist manifesto and exhibits geometric abstract paintings*	•*ANZAC troops slaughtered on Gallipoli* •*British passenger ship* Lusitania *torpedoed*	•*Matte Truco's reinforced concrete Lingotto car factory, Turin, Italy*	•*D. W. Griffith's U.S. civil war epic,* The Birth of a Nation •*Cecil B. De Mille:* The Cheat	•*Death of soldier-poet Rupert Brooke* •*Ford Madox Ford:* The Good Soldier
1916	•*Boccioni, Franz Marc, and Sant'Elia killed in action* •*Dada born in Cabaret Voltaire, Zurich*	•*Ireland: Easter Rising in Dublin* •*Battles of Verdun and the Somme*	•*Johnston's sans serif typeface for the London Underground*	•*Lillian Gish stars in D. W. Griffith's second silent epic,* Intolerance	•*Franz Kafka:* Metamorphosis •*Albert Einstein:* General Theory of Relativity
1917	•*Duchamp's ready-made sculpture,* Fountain •*Carrà and de Chirico launch Metaphysical Painting*	•*Revolution in Russia; Lenin takes power* •*Brazil and U.S. declare war on Germany*	•*Mondrian and van Doesburg start De Stijl movement*	•*Mary Pickford stars in* The Poor Little Rich Girl •*Charlie Chaplin stars in* The Immigrant	•*Henry Handel Richardson:* Australia Felix •*Erik Satie's* Parade *for the Russian Ballet*
1918	•*Malevich's white on white series* •*Death of Klimt*	•*Armistice ends World War I* •*Britain: women over 30 get the vote*	•*De Stijl designer Gerrit Rietveld's Red and Blue armchair*	•*Vladimir Mayakovsky's pro-revolution play,* Mystery-Bouffe, *first performed in Russia*	•*Booth Tarkington:* The Magnificent Ambersons •*Siegfried Sassoon's anti-war poems,* Counterattack
1919	•*Death of Auguste Renoir* •*Mondrian returns to Paris*	•*Treaty of Versailles between Allies and Germany* •*Germany: Hitler becomes leader of Nazi Party*	•*Bauhaus design school founded in Germany by Walter Gropius*	•*Robert Wiene's Expressionist film,* The Cabinet of Dr. Caligari •*United Artists founded*	•*Virginia Woolf:* Night and Day •*André Gide:* Two Symphonies

GLOSSARY

abstract art: art that does not attempt to portray its subjects as they are seen in the real world. Abstract artists seek to express meaning or emotions through shapes and colors.

absurd: ridiculous; having no foundation in reason.

avant-garde: having, or pioneering, the development of, new, bold, or experimental styles or techniques.

collage: artwork consisting of scraps of material, such as paper, cloth, or string, glued onto a surface.

chaos: a state of confusion and disorder.

drafted: ordered by the government to join the military.

geometric abstraction: the creation of abstract art based on geometric shapes, such as rectangles, circles, or triangles.

jagged: having a rough, uneven edge or quality.

Impressionism: an art movement that originated in the late 1860s. Its followers painted "impressions" of everyday scenes and tried to quickly capture the fleeting effects of light reflecting off surfaces.

propaganda: ideas spread purposely to gain support for a cause or to damage or defeat an opposing cause.

perspective: the illusion of three dimensions created on a flat, two-dimensional surface.

ready-made: the name given by Marcel Duchamp to manufactured objects he and other artists chose at random and presented as works of art.

representational: the quality of portraying an object as it is seen in real life.

Surrealism: an art movement that stressed the importance of using dreams and the unconscious mind to create art.

MORE BOOKS TO READ

1900-20: The Birth of Modernism. 20th Century Design (series). Jackie Gaff (Gareth Stevens)

The 1910s. Cultural History of the United States Through the Decades (series). Michael V. Uschan, editor (Lucent Books)

The Blue Rider: The Yellow Cow Sees the World in Blue. Adventures in Art (series). Doris Kutschbach and Andrea P. A. Belloli (Prestel USA)

De Chirico: The Metaphysical Period, 1888-1919. Paolo Baldacci, Giorgio de Chirico, and Jeffrey Jennings, translator (Bulfinch Press)

Kazimir Malevich. Masters of Art (series). Charlotte Douglas and Kazimir Severinovich Malevich (Harry N. Abrams)

Modigliani. Great Modern Masters (series). Amedeo Modigliani; Alberto Curotto, translator; and Jose Maria Faerna, editor (Abradale Press)

Piet Mondrian 1872-1944: Structures in Space. Basic Art (series). Susanne Deicher and Piet Mondrian (Taschen America)

Rodchenko: Photography 1924-1954. Alexander Lavrentiev, editor (Konemann)

31

WEB SITES

Art of the First World War.
www.art-ww1.com/gb/peintre.html

Italian Futurist Artists.
www.futurism.fsnet.co.uk/artists.htm

DaDa Online
www.peak.org/~dadaist/English/Graphics/index.html

Piet Mondrian Resources and Links
www.fmf.nl/~jeldert/hendrik/mondriaan/resource.html

Due to the dynamic nature of the Internet, some web sites stay current longer than others. To find additional web sites, use a reliable search engine with one or more of the following keywords: *abstract art, Constructivism, Cubism, DaDa, Futurism, Metaphysical Painting, Suprematism, Vorticism, World War I art*, and the names of individual artists.

INDEX